GENERATING
ELECTRICITY

GREGORY VOGT

GENERATING ELECTRICITY

A GROLIER COMPANY

FRANKLIN WATTS
NEW YORK ■ LONDON ■ TORONTO ■ SYDNEY ■ 1986
A FIRST BOOK

Diagrams by Vantage Art

Photographs courtesy of
Department of Energy: 29, 33, 48;
UPI/Bettmann Newsphotos: p. 2;
Bakken Library of Electricity in Life: p. 5;
Con Edison: p. 18; AP/Wide World: p. 27;
NASA: p. 59.

Library of Congress Cataloging in Publication Data

Vogt, Gregory.
Generating electricity.

(A First book)
Bibliography: p.
Includes index.
Summary: Describes how common and uncommon forms
of electricity are produced or generated. Includes
instructions for several experiments and a glossary
of terms.
1. Electricity—Juvenile literature. 2. Electricity
—Experiments—Juvenile literature. 3. Electric
generators—Juvenile literature. [1. Electricity.
2. Electricity—Experiments. 3. Experiments]
I. Title.
QC527.2.V643   1986   621.31   85-20202
ISBN 0-531-10117-7

CONTENTS

INTRODUCTION

If you were to try to count all the ways you use electricity, you would be in for a major task. Electricity is at the very core of modern-day life. It is used to run motors, televisions, lights, refrigerators, clocks, calculators, and computers. It is used in making paper, clothing, automobiles, food packaging, furniture, and toys. The list goes on and on.

Our dependency upon electricity is the result of the ease with which it is produced. To use electricity, all you have to do is flip a switch and it is there at your command. This availability has encouraged thousands of inventors to invent thousands of devices that use electricity.

How electricity is generated, or produced, is the subject of this book. You will learn the most common forms of electrical generation along with some pretty unusual forms of generation as well. Because learning by experience is always best, several experiments you can do will be presented also.

This woman is touching a Van de Graaff generator. You probably experience the effects of static electricity in less dramatic ways, for example, when you touch a doorknob after walking on carpet on a dry day.

ELECTRICITY

On a cold winter day when the air inside your house is very dry, you walk across the room to the door. Reaching out to the metal doorknob, you momentarily stop when you feel an irritating though not too painful snap at your finger. A spark has leaped out from your finger to the doorknob.

On that same dry day, rubbing the back of a cat or a dog produces all sorts of snaps and crackles—and tiny blue flashes if it's dark. Clothes pulled straight from the clothes drier crackle when separated. Each of these events is part of the fascinating world of electricity. In each, you participated in generating electric charges that leaped out as sparks of electric current.

Electricity has been generated ever since the world began. The friction between water and ice particles in storm clouds can produce tremendous electric charges that leap between the clouds or between the clouds and the land below in powerful lightning bolts.

Although ages ago people began generating electricity by rubbing their hair, the first person to take proper note of the effects rubbing produced was probably Thales, a Greek astronomer who lived about 2,500 years ago. Thales observed that amber (in his day it was called "elektron") gained an attractive power similar to magnetism when it was rubbed with fur. Amber is tree sap that has turned to stone. Following rubbing, the amber attracted things like tiny bits of paper and lint. Thales mistakenly believed the amber was alive because it attracted these materials as though it were breathing and sucking in air. The real cause of the attraction was the generation of *static electricity* by rubbing the amber with the fur.

FROM VON GUERICKE
TO FARADAY

Following Thales, more than 2,000 years passed before the first machines for generating static electricity were invented. In 1660, Otto von Guericke built a machine that produced electricity using a spinning ball of sulfur. With the static charge generated, von Guericke was able to demonstrate the same attractive effects that Thales had noted; crackling noises, sparks, and even a strange odor in the air. Many other scientists followed von Guericke's example by building static electricity generators. They, too, began to experiment with static electricity.

In 1800, Alessandro Volta stacked small alternating piles of silver and zinc disks separated with paper or cloth soaked in saltwater. Volta noted that the piles produced electricity. This was the invention of the first chemical battery.

In 1820, Hans Christian Oersted of the University of Copenhagen conducted a classic experiment for his students that demonstrated a relationship between magnetism and electricity. Oersted placed a wire over a compass with its needle parallel to the wire. He ran an electric current, produced from a battery similar to the one Volta invented, through the wire. The current produced a magnetic field that caused the compass needle to move perpendicular to the wire. In other words, the electric current produced a magnetic field around the wire that affected the compass needle.

From Oersted's work it was a small but important step to reversing the process and using magnetism to produce electricity. Michael Faraday conducted an experiment in 1830 that did just this. Faraday wrapped wire around a welded iron ring. The ends of the wire were connected to a galvanometer (the same kind of device used by Oersted), a device that indicates the passage of an electric current

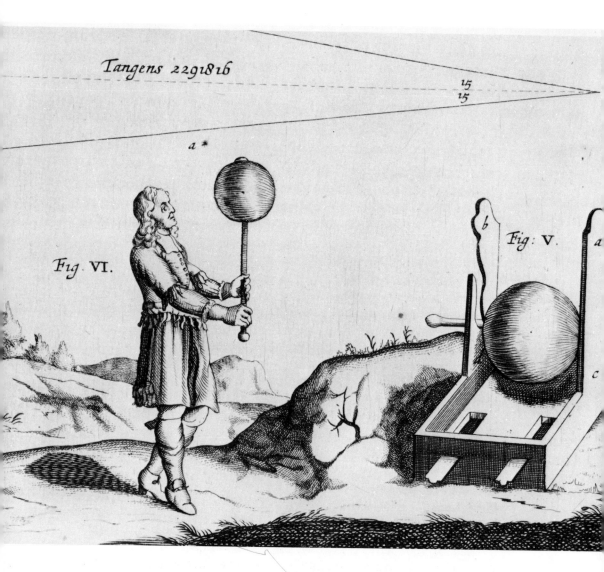

Otto von Guericke's static generator. If the large ball is charged, what do you think will happen when the man touches it with the smaller ball?

with the movement of a needle. When Faraday passed a strong magnet through the ring, he noted that the needle moved. When the magnet was retracted, the needle moved again. The electric current was generated only when the magnet moved.

The scientific research of Thales, von Guericke, Volta, Oersted, Faraday, and other early scientists resulted in the discoveries about electricity that so much of our twentieth-century lifestyle depends upon. Yet, none of those scientists understood what electricity was. They could describe what electricity did, but did not know what it consisted of. A basic understanding of what electricity was, started with the discovery of the parts of the atom, a process that began at the end of the nineteenth century and is still continuing today.

EXPERIMENT:
CHARGING BALLOONS WITH
STATIC ELECTRICITY

Static electricity experiments work best in the winter when the air is very dry. Charging the balloon in the summer is much harder because moisture in the air leaks away electrons.

MATERIALS

Two balloons
String
Silk, wool, or fur
Puffed rice

Rub one of the balloons with the silk, wool, or fur. Rubbing charges the balloon with static electricity. Bring the charged balloon near the puffed rice. If the balloon is charged, the puffed rice will jump into the air and stick to it. Try touching the charged balloon to a wall and letting it go. Bring the charged balloon near your hair.

Take the second balloon and tie a string around the nozzle. Rub this balloon to charge it also. Hold this balloon by the string and try to touch it with the other charged balloon.

Why do the charged balloons attract the puffed rice, the wall, and your hair but repel each other?

Rubbing the balloon transfers loose electrons from the silk, wool, or fur to the surface of the balloon. This gives the balloon a negative charge.

When a charged balloon is brought near the puffed rice, some of the electrons in the rice are repelled to their other sides. This leaves their near sides positively charged. Positive charges attract negative charges, and the rice sticks to the balloon. A similar attraction takes place between the balloon and the wall and between the balloon and your hair.

When two negatively charged balloons come near each other, they push each other apart. Negative charges repel negative charges.

ELECTRICITY
BEGINS
WITH ATOMS

To understand how electricity is generated, it is valuable to understand what electricity is. To do that, we must descend into inner space, into the heart of the atom.

All matter is made up of atoms. They are the tiny building blocks, only one one-hundred-millionth of an inch in diameter (about three one-hundred-millionths of a centimeter), that make up the entire universe. Atoms themselves are made up of even smaller building blocks, called subatomic particles—protons, neutrons, and electrons. The protons and neutrons reside in the center of the atom, and the electrons surround the center (Fig. 1).

Protons and electrons each have what scientists call an electric charge. Protons have a positive charge, electrons a negative charge. These opposite charges attract each other. Later, we will see how important this attraction is.

ELECTRIC CURRENT

In many materials, such as most metals, some of the outer electrons circling the atoms are shared between atoms. In other words, for a time, an electron will circle one atom and then circle another. This is just their normal state. However, if these jumping electrons can be made to all jump in the same direction at the same time, then a stream, or current, of electrons is produced. This is called *electric current*.

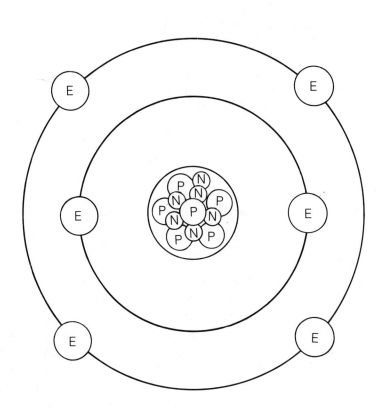

Fig. 1. In a typical atom, represented here, the protons and neutrons cluster in the center while the electrons surround the nucleus.

Although electric currents can travel through air as lightning does, their usual pathway is through conductors. A conductor is a material that provides an easy pathway for electricity to travel. Copper wire is an excellent conductor of electricity, and so are silver and gold. Lead, on the other hand, is a very poor conductor.

There also must be a complete circuit, or "circle," for the electricity to travel in. The wire has to form a loop, or else electrons will pile up at one end of the wire while the other end becomes short of electrons. The two ends become charged positive and negative, and the electrons will immediately return to where they came from because positive charges attract negative charges. Keeping the electrons flowing requires a continual push on them while at the same time giving them a place to go.

STATIC ELECTRICITY

A second kind of electricity also involves electrons. Sometimes, the jumping electrons collect on the surface of some object. The electrons come to rest in a condition called static electricity. Remember, electrons have negative charges. Negative charges repel each other. As more electrons gather on the surface, the pressure of the electrons on each other becomes very great. If something comes near the object, the electrons can release that pressure and leap through the air as an electric current. This is what happens when you drag your feet across a carpet in winter and then reach out to a metal doorknob. By rubbing your feet, you collect electrons on the surface of your body and build up a charge of static electricity. The pressure of the electrons is released when they leap through the air to the doorknob.

Static electricity was the kind of electricity produced by Thales many years ago when he rubbed amber with fur. By rubbing, electrons from the fur transferred to the surface of the amber and came to rest. The amber became negatively charged because of the excess of electrons resting on its surface. This negative charge attracted lightweight materials.

EXPERIMENT:
MAKING
AN ELECTROPHORUS

The electrophorus, invented by Alessandro Volta in 1775, is a simple device for producing static electricity.

MATERIALS

Metal jar lid
Wax candle
Old phonograph record or sheet of hard plastic
Piece of wool, flannel, or fur
Sandpaper
Fluorescent lamp tube

Sand the paint off the outside of the jar lid and remove any paper or plastic inside the lid. Clean the lid thoroughly.

Light the candle and drip wax into the center of the lid. Stick the bottom of the candle into the wax and hold it there until it hardens (Fig. 2).

Place the record or plastic on a flat surface and rub it vigorously with the wool, flannel, or fur. Hold the lid by the candle and set it on the record or plastic. Touch the bare surface of the lid with your finger. After a few seconds, remove your finger and lift the lid with the candle. Now bring your finger near the lid again, and a spark should leap from your finger to the lid. You can repeat this over and over.

What causes the spark?

Rubbing the record or plastic transfers electrons to its surface, giving it a negative charge. Setting the lid on the record or plastic brings these two surfaces close together. The electrons in the record or plastic repel electrons in the lid and makes them move upward. When you touch the lid, electrons move onto your finger. Now the lid has a shortage of electrons and is positively charged. When you

Fig. 2. The completed electrophorus described in the text.

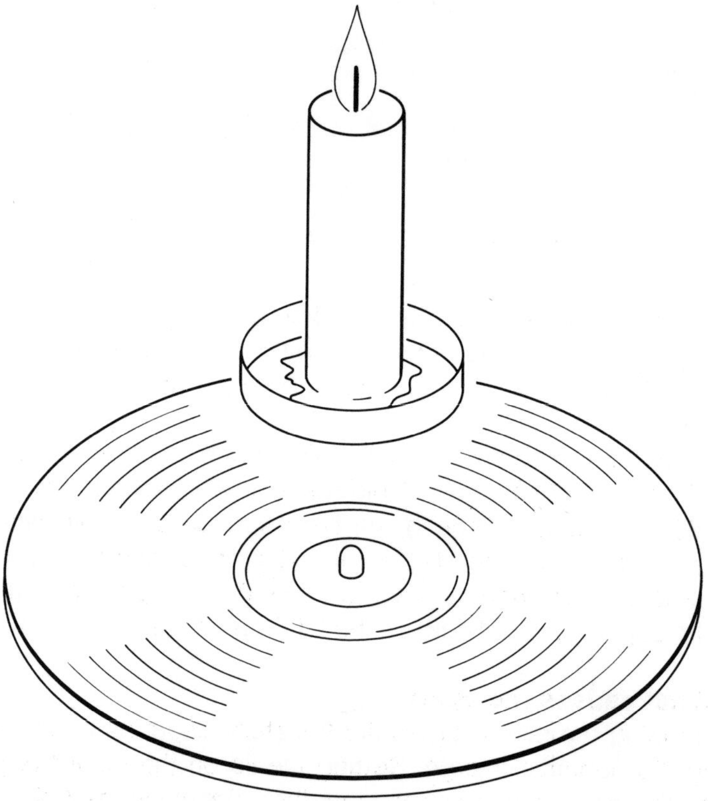

bring the lid near your finger again, electrons leap out from your finger as a spark and hit the lid. The lid is no longer charged.

Do the next part of the experiment only under supervision. Take your electrophorus into a room that can be made very dark. Charge it again and watch the spark as it leaves your finger. Charge it again and this time bring it near the end of a fluorescent tube. The tube flickers for a few moments.

Why does the tube light up?

When electricity passes through a fluorescent tube, the electrons jump between the atoms in the thin gas inside. As an electron moves into orbit about an atom, it gives off a tiny bit of light for an instant.

The weak light you see when you bring a charged object near the tube is produced by the moving electrons inside the tube. Electrons move inside the tube toward the electrophorus, and some of them jump through the air. More electrons enter the other end of the tube from your finger to neutralize the tube again.

MACHINES THAT GENERATE ELECTRICITY

STATIC ELECTRICITY GENERATORS

The earliest generators were strange contraptions that generated weak static electric charges. They were built because scientists who wanted to study electricity had to have a way to produce large amounts of electricity whenever they wanted it. In von Guericke's machine, described earlier, a large ball of sulfur was rotated by a crank. A person touched the ball, and the rubbing produced by the rotation removed electrons from the hand and transferred them to the ball. Another person received the electrons by touching the ball and, in doing so, gained a static charge. Some experimenters suspended the second person from the ceiling in a sling!

Another static generator, the Wimshurst machine, was invented in 1878. It consisted of two glass disks that rotated in opposite directions. Each disk had many copper plates attached. As the disks rotated in opposite directions, small metal strips rubbed the plates. In doing so, electrons were transferred from the strips to the plates. These electrons would then be picked up at another point on the disks and moved to a storage jar that would temporarily hold the charge.

To keep electrons moving through the machine, a second jar had to yield some of its electrons. In doing so, it became positively charged. When the two jars each built up a strong static charge, one positive and the other negative, a strong spark of electricity leaped through the air from the negative jar to the positive jar across a gap between two metal rods. At that moment, everything would become neutral again until new static charges built up by continued rotation of the disk. The Wimshurst machine was used in the late 1890s to power X-ray machines for doctors' offices.

Robert Van de Graaff invented a static electricity generator in 1929 that was much more powerful than the Wimshurst machine. It was named the Van de Graaff generator.

A Van de Graaff generator begins with a leather or rubber belt that runs vertically between two pulleys. Electrons are picked up on the lower end of the belt and carried to the upper end, where they get off and move to the inside of a metal ball. Then the electrons immediately move to the outside of the ball because their negative charges repel one another. The outer surface of the ball has more surface area for them to move to. Eventually, the charge on the out-side of the ball becomes so great that it leaps outward to some nearby object.

Van de Graaff generators can produce a very high voltage, but the actual number of electrons in that current is small so that dis-charges of smaller Van de Graaff generators are relatively harmless. Many school science classrooms use this kind of generator because it can produce spectacular static electricity effects, such as making people's hair stand on end, without harming them. Large Van de Graaff generators of this type have been used to power X-ray machines and atom smashers, devices that split apart atoms so that scientists can study the pieces.

MAGNETIC GENERATORS

Most of the electricity that we use every day is produced by *magnetic generators*. A magnetic generator takes advantage of Michael Faraday's discovery in 1830 that certain movements of a magnet near a coil of wire produce an electric current in the wire. As long as the magnet is kept in constant motion, the current continues. Moving the wire instead of the magnet also produces a current.

Magnetic generators in use by electric power companies are large and weigh many tons, but we can understand how these generators work by examining small generators. Essentially, a magnetic generator is just a coil of wire that is made to rotate between strong magnets (Fig. 3). During the rotation, electrons in the wire are propelled along the wire by the force of the magnets. These moving electrons become an electric current.

In order to enable the current to leave the generator so that it can be put to use, the ends of the wire coil are joined to two separate metal rings that circle the axle of the coil. Small strips of metal, called *brushes,* touch these rings. This arrangement provides a pathway for the electricity to travel.

As the coil spins, the direction the electricity travels constantly changes. The magnets propel electrons through the wire in the coil in only one direction. However, the coil keeps turning over because it is rotating. During one half of a turn, the electricity travels one direction through the coil. During the other half, it travels in the other direction. This is called *alternating current (AC).*

A second kind of magnetic generator produces electricity that travels in one direction only. This is called *direct current (DC)* (Fig. 4). This kind of generator is very similar to the first one described. The main difference is in the metal rings that the brushes rub against during turning. In a direct current generator there is only one ring and it is cut into two pieces. One end of the wire coil is joined to each piece.

Each brush touches only one ring piece at a time. As the coil rotates, the brushes touch one ring piece and then the other, over and over. In an AC generator, the current direction changes as the coil is rotated. But with this generator, contact with the brushes and the ring pieces is broken just before the current can change direction. New contacts are made and again broken just before the direction change takes place. This keeps the current flowing out of the generator traveling in one direction only.

Generators used by electric power companies are usually of the alternating current variety. Instead of placing large magnets on the

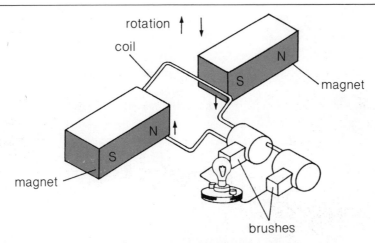

Fig. 3. As the coil in an alternating current generator turns, the electricity produced changes directions in the wire each time the coil flips over.

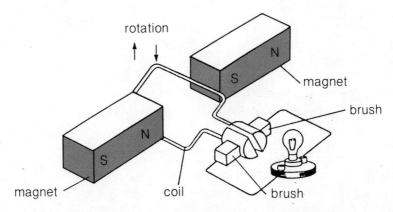

Fig. 4. As the coil in a direct current generator turns, the electricity produced travels in one direction only. The ring pieces make and break contact with the brushes before the current can change direction.

A modern magnetic generator.

outside of the generators, they use large coils of wire. Electricity is passed through these coils, turning them into a powerful magnet. The field of this magnet is sufficient to produce an electric current in the rotating coil inside.

To get the large power company generators started, an electric current from another generator must be run through the outer coils. After the generator is able to produce electricity on its own, some of that electricity can be used to keep a current running through its own outer coils.

One point about magnetic generators hasn't been addressed yet. What causes the rotor to turn? Some form of machine is connected to the rotor shaft, and when the machine turns, so does the rotor. The driving force behind this machine can be many things. It can be falling water, high-pressure steam, or moving air. The driving forces will be described in the next chapter.

EXPERIMENT:
MAKING AN ELECTRIC SWING

Faraday's discovery can be demonstrated in this simple experiment. With some magnets, wire, and wood, you will be able to make a magnetic generator and an electric motor.

MATERIALS

Two large horseshoe magnets (you should be able to borrow these at school)
75 feet (23 m) of bell wire
4 boards, about 1 x 1 x 20 inches (2.5 x 2.5 x 51 cm)
1 board, about 6 x 1 x 20 inches (15 x 2.5 x 51 cm)
Several nails

Wind two coils of wire fifty turns each, about 3 inches (7.6 cm) in diameter. Set up the wood frame as shown in Fig. 5. Suspend the

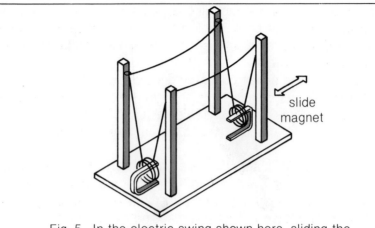

Fig. 5. In the electric swing shown here, sliding the magnet in and out of the wire coil generates an electric current. The current travels to the second coil, magnetizing it. The second coil is then either repelled from or attracted to the second magnet.

coils so the magnets will slide freely inside the coils. Connect the wires so that electricity can circle from one coil to the next.

When the electric swing is ready, slide one of the magnets in and out of its coil. Try not to shake the platform. Watch what happens to the second coil.

Why does the second coil move?

The electric swing is actually a combination of a magnetic generator and an electric motor. When you move one magnet, the field of that magnet repels electrons in the nearby coil and starts an electric current. This is the principle of the magnetic generator. The electrons circle through the two wire coils as long as the magnet is moving.

When the current runs through the second coil, it produces a magnetic field. That field interacts with the field of the second magnet. The two fields either attract each other and the coil swings inward or they repel and the coil swings away. Movement caused by electromagnetism is the principle of the electric motor.

STEAM-GENERATED POWER

Most of the electricity we use every day comes from steam-propelled magnetic generators. Water is heated until it expands greatly to form steam. The pressure produced by the expanding steam spins a turbine, which then turns a magnetic generator.

Producing the heat for making steam can be done in many ways. Anything that burns can be used to heat the water, including coal, oil, natural gas, even trash. Water also can be turned into steam from the heat produced in a nuclear power reactor by the breaking apart, or fissioning, of certain elements. No matter what heat source is used, the heat is added to water in a high-pressure boiler. The steam produced has more force when it is sent to the turbine. The blades of the turbine look a bit like waterwheels but are designed to be much more efficient. The steam expands explosively as it pushes on the turbine blades. The energy of the flowing steam pushes the turbine blades, whose motion turns the generator (Fig. 6).

FOSSIL FUELS

Among the most common substances burned to produce electricity are fossil fuels. Fossil fuels are the product of many millions of years of accumulation of plants and animals that lived in swamps and the seas. Upon death, their remains piled up and eventually changed into coal, oil, or natural gas. Today, we mine or drill for these fossil fuels because they are an important source of heat that can be used for, among other things, generating electricity.

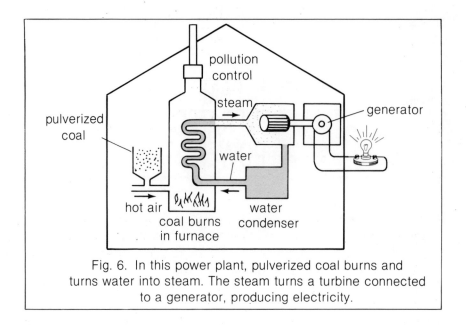

Fig. 6. In this power plant, pulverized coal burns and turns water into steam. The steam turns a turbine connected to a generator, producing electricity.

Coal is the most commonly used fossil fuel for generating electricity. The reason for this is cost. Both oil and natural gas cost more than coal. As a result, approximately 50 percent of our daily electricity supplies comes from coal generation. Only about 16 percent comes from burning oil and 14 percent from burning natural gas.

Usually, coal is first ground into small particles before being blown into the furnace and burned. Small pieces of coal release more energy than big pieces when burned. Oil, on the other hand, is just sprayed into the furnace, and natural gas comes in through jets.

In some coal systems, the coal is turned into a sludgelike oil in a process called liquefaction. The oil is burned in an oil furnace. In another process—*coal gasification*—coal is turned into a gas, which is burned in natural-gas furnaces.

Coal plants have some drawbacks. For one thing, pollution goes up the smokestacks from the furnaces. Power companies go to great lengths and spend large amounts of money to clean the smoke, made of tiny soot particles, that comes from burning coal. However, they often have trouble removing sulfur dioxide gases that come from burning some forms of coal. In the air, sulfur dioxide combines with water to make acid rain, which damages living things and buildings and may produce long-term major damage to our world.

Another drawback is getting the coal in the first place and still another is what to do with the ash left over from burning it. Much coal is mined from large pits that scar the earth's surface. The damages can be repaired by relandscaping the mine site. Other coal mines are below ground and can be very dangerous to work in. Strict rules must be followed to make underground mines relatively safe. The ash left after burning coal can be used as a filler in making building blocks and other construction materials.

Oil can be a much cleaner fuel to burn than coal, although some oil has a high sulfur content. Burning high-sulfur oil can also contribute to the acid rain problem.

Natural gas is the cleanest-burning fuel. It is so clean-burning that it is used as fuel in millions of home kitchen stoves. Unfortunately, natural gas is in much shorter supply than coal and therefore much more expensive.

NUCLEAR FUELS

With the explosion of the first atomic bombs in the 1940s, people became aware that a new power had been released on earth, an awesome power with two faces. One face was destructive on an unimaginable scale and the other was constructive, with the potential of great benefit to all people. Among other benefits, the energy within the atom itself could be released and used to generate electricity.

Today, many electric power plants take advantage of the controlled release of energy from atoms. These plants are called nuclear *power plants* because the energy they use comes right from the nucleus of the atoms themselves.

Inside a nuclear power plant is a *reactor*, the place where the energy of the atom is released. The reactor is filled with radioactive atoms, which are unstable and will decay in time into some other kind of atom. An atom becomes unstable when the number of protons and the number of neutrons in the nucleus of the atom are very different from each other. Most atoms have similar numbers of protons and neutrons, but when the numbers are very different, such as in uranium, the result is an unstable atom. A typical example of an unstable atom is uranium 238. This form of uranium is considered the natural form because it is the most common. It has 92 protons and 146 neutrons. Another form of uranium is uranium 235, which has 92 protons and 143 neutrons. It is found in very small quantities along with uranium 238.

Uranium 235 will undergo a special process called *fission*. It will break apart under severe stress. When atoms undergo fission, they break apart into two smaller atoms and release two or three neutrons along with a large amount of heat.

If a large number of uranium atoms are placed near each other, some of the neutrons from the fissioning of one atom may strike the nucleus of others. When this happens, the struck atom splits into two roughly equal pieces, with one, two, or three additional neutrons flying off. These neutrons may strike other nuclei, and they too will split. From this, you can see that more and more uranium atoms will be split. This ever increasing number of fissions is called a chain reaction. Tremendous amounts of heat are released during the reaction. If uncontrolled, a gigantic nuclear explosion results. If controlled, in a nuclear power plant reactor, useful heat is released. This heat can be turned to steam that will turn turbines connected to magnetic electric generators (Fig. 7).

Within the nuclear power plant reactor, concentrated pellets of uranium 235 fuel are placed inside a large water-filled kettle called the reactor vessel. The water helps keep the heat produced by the uranium fuel under control.

Uranium fuel pellets are small cylinders less than 1 inch (2.5 cm) long and about the diameter of a pencil. One pellet contains the energy equivalent of almost 1 ton of coal (about 910 kg). A typical nuclear power reactor might hold more than five million pellets. They are packed inside long metal tubes called fuel rods and are positioned in bundles to form a core inside the reactor.

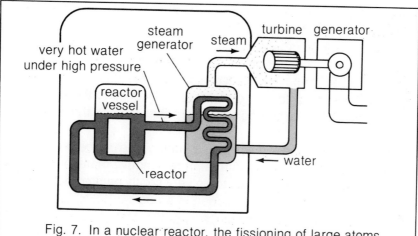

Fig. 7. In a nuclear reactor, the fissioning of large atoms into smaller ones releases heat that creates steam by boiling water. The steam drives a turbine that turns the generator.

In between the fuel rods are control rods that can capture the neutrons and prevent the neutrons from splitting uranium atoms in other fuel rods. When the control rods are pulled away, the neutrons from fissioning uranium atoms can strike other uranium atoms at other parts in the vessel and the chain reaction begins. Heat from the reaction boils water in a system of pipes. The steam produced turns turbines which turn a generator that produces electricity.

Nuclear power plants are the most controversial of all power plants. Because they use dangerous radioactive atoms, many safeguards have to be taken to protect the public from potential dangers. Danger comes primarily from the radioactive waste products that result when the fuel is exhausted. How this waste is disposed of is a major public concern. Some of the waste remains dangerous for thousands of years. Most ideas for storing the waste propose deep burial in the earth, such as placing the wastes in deep mines and then sealing the mines. Not just any mine will do. The mines have to be in very stable areas of the world that have few earthquakes. An earthquake can break open a storage mine and release the wastes into the environment.

Another problem with nuclear power is the disposal of waste heat after the steam has been used to turn the turbine. Sometimes, nuclear power plants are placed along shorelines of large lakes or rivers and use the cold lake or river water for cooling the waste heat. Other plants build large cooling towers that release the heat to the atmosphere.

A third safety problem is more an unrealistic concern than a real danger: nuclear explosions. Although radioactive material is used in these plants, that material has to be very tightly packed before it can explode. This just does not happen in a nuclear power plant.

Nuclear power plants produce approximately 13 percent of the electricity used in the United States. This percentage is not likely to increase in the near future because of the high cost. A nuclear power plant is very complex, and builders must abide by many safety regulations and environmental safeguards. Materials to build these plants are expensive, and construction can take many years. These factors have driven the cost of nuclear power plants up to $4 or $5 billion. That cost can bankrupt an electric power company building the plant.

GEOTHERMAL ENERGY

The earth is a large chunk of rock some 8,000 miles (about 12,900 km) in diameter. Miners who have dug very deep shafts into the earth have noticed that as they go deeper, the temperature of the rock rises. It rises approximately 1 degree Fahrenheit (about ½ degree Celsius) every 35 or so feet (about 10 m) or 150 degrees Fahrenheit per mile (about 83 degrees Celsius for every 1.6 km). At a

Engineers studying pressure and temperatures of a geothermal steam well at the Geysers Power Plant in Sonoma County, California.

depth greater than a mile and a half (about 2.4 km), the rock temperatures can be so high as to boil drops of water that come into contact with it. The change in temperature is due to pressure and natural radioactive decay of certain elements. Very deep mines need cooling systems to protect the miners from the heat.

Heat from pressure and radioactive decay in the earth is called *geothermal heat.* Under the right conditions, it can be tapped to turn water into steam to turn turbines connected to magnetic electric generators. Unfortunately, the right conditions are relatively rare. You don't just drill a hole a mile and a half deep and then expect to use the heat at the bottom to make electricity. The hole is so deep that by the time the steam has been brought to the surface, it already has cooled and is useless for turning turbines.

The right conditions for geothermal power are found in areas of the earth which have frequent volcanic and earthquake activity. Iceland is one such place, and so are Hawaii and parts of California. In each of these places, the great interior heat of the earth is much nearer the surface. In some locations, steam is formed from groundwater that has naturally seeped into the earth and shoots out through natural vents. If the steam is under high enough pressure, it can be caught and used to produce electricity. If not, holes are drilled into the hot zones and pipes lowered into them. Water is pumped into one hole, and the resulting steam comes up through a second hole.

Geothermal electricity is one of the cleanest forms of generating electricity because little pollution is produced by it. Unfortunately, few places are suitable for geothermal plants. At present, less than 1 percent of the United States' electricity supplies comes from geothermal power.

SOLAR THERMAL SYSTEMS

Another way of producing steam from water that does not involve burning is the use of the heat from the sun. Using the sun in this manner is still very experimental, but it has great potential for the future.

A solar thermal electric plant in Barstow,
California (see text for description).

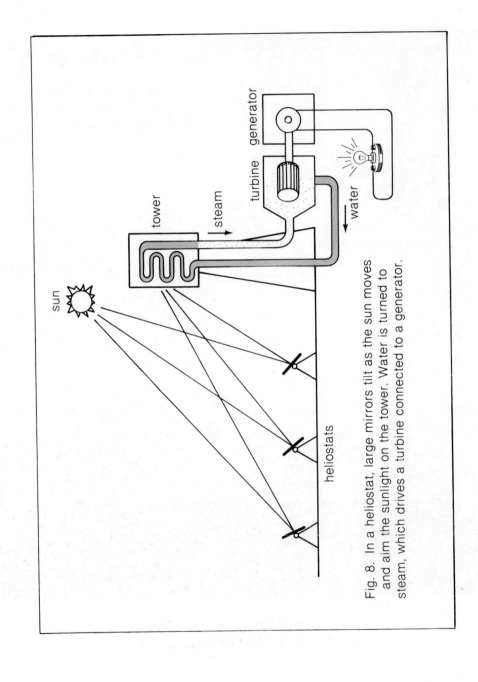

Fig. 8. In a heliostat, large mirrors tilt as the sun moves and aim the sunlight on the tower. Water is turned to steam, which drives a turbine connected to a generator.

A solar thermal generator can work only with sunlight that has been concentrated since very high temperatures are needed to produce steam. You have probably used a magnifying glass to concentrate sunlight to burn paper and leaves. Lenses are not practical for most solar thermal generators because of the problem of size. To make the generator practical, the sunlight that falls on acres of land must be concentrated. A lens that size would be far too heavy to be supported, and it would always have to be moved so that its surface was perpendicular to the sun's rays. This would require a huge and expensive machine to move it.

Research and testing are going on with mirror systems for solar thermal generators. One intriguing design calls for hundreds of individual flat mirrors, called *heliostats*, each mounted on its own movable base (Fig. 8). Each mirror can be made of smaller mirrors grouped together to produce large-surface mirrors approximately 20 feet (6 m) on a side. A machine points the reflective side of the mirrors in nearly a direct line with the sun and keeps it in line all day long. The reflection from the mirror is aimed at the top of a tall tower directly to the south.

Because this system can have hundreds of mirrors—each with its own drive machine, each sending the sun's light to the top of the tower—a tremendous amount of solar heat is concentrated in one relatively small area. This has the same effect as using a magnifying lens to burn leaves.

At the top of the tower is a boiler. Water is injected into the boiler, heated by the concentrated sunlight, and quickly turned into high-pressure steam. The steam is piped to a turbine, which turns because of the expanding steam. The turbine spins the generator, and electricity is produced.

The biggest problem with solar thermal plants is where to locate them. Areas that receive little sunlight, because of frequent clouds, are not suited to solar thermal generator systems. And since they work only during the day, a system is required to store the electricity. Solar thermal systems also require a large surface area on which to be built.

WIND- AND WATER-GENERATED POWER

Electricity can also be produced by generators turned by water and wind. Since nothing has to be burned to produce the steam needed to turn the generator, wind and water power are much cleaner forms of energy than energy produced by the burning of fossil fuels or by nuclear fission.

WIND GENERATORS

Wind is one of the earliest forms of energy humans used for doing work because it was so easy to use. All that was necessary was to hold up something to catch it with. A boat with large sails was easily propelled by the power of the captured wind. A large propeller made of sails or blades rotated when the wind blew and produced turning power for grinding grain. Today, wind is also being put to use for turning magnetic generators.

Wind is simply air in motion. The energy to make air move comes from the sun and from the earth's rotation. Wind energy can really be thought of as another form of solar thermal power. The sun's heat warms the air above the earth's surface, causing it to rise. Cooler air from somewhere else rushes in to fill the place left by the rising hot air. That rushing air is wind. At night and during the winter—and other times too—there is little heating of the air and the air cools off. Cool air contracts and becomes more dense. It falls to the surface of the earth. Rather than pile up on the surface, the cool air spreads out

A wind turbine located in Goldendale, Washington.
The blade is 300 feet (91m) long, the tower is
200 feet (61m) high. This wind generator produces
2.5 million watts of electricity in winds of 14 miles
per hour (23 kmph) to 45 miles per hour (72 kmph).

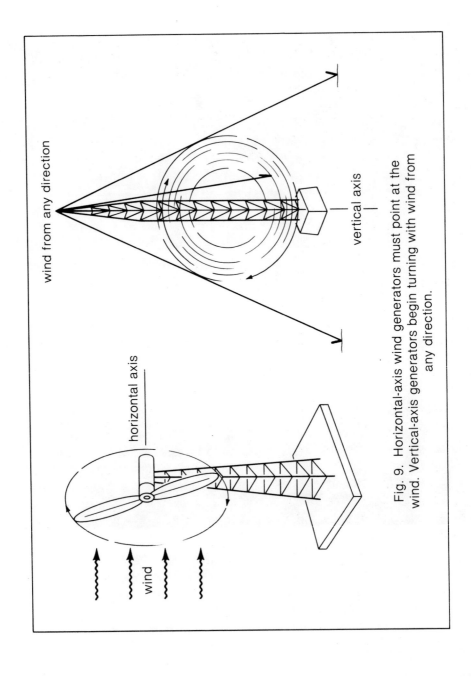

wind from any direction

vertical axis

horizontal axis

wind

Fig. 9. Horizontal-axis wind generators must point at the wind. Vertical-axis generators begin turning with wind from any direction.

over the earth's surface in rushing air currents of wind. Because the earth's surface is covered with warm and cool spots, air is constantly rising or falling, producing wind.

All this moving air around the world can be put to use by wind generators for generating electricity. Wind generators have some sort of propeller with blades or large scoops that rotate when the wind blows. They capture the wind in much the same way as water-wheels catch running water. The rotation turns a magnetic generator that produces the electric current.

Wind generators come in two kinds: those that spin with a horizontal axis, and those that have a vertical axis (Fig. 9). Vertical-axis wind generators spin like a top when the wind blows. The wind can come from any direction, giving them a distinct advantage over the other kind. Horizontal-axis windmills have to point into the wind first before they can work. They use some of the wind's energy in just pointing themselves.

Normally, the blades of vertical-axis windmills are scoop-shaped, giving them the appearance of a large spinning drum, although some varieties look more like eggbeaters. Their spin is transferred by a chain drive or a gear drive system to the generator.

The big disadvantage of vertical-axis wind generators is size. As a general rule, with wind power, each time you double the diameter of a wind generator, the electric power generated is multiplied four times. Therefore, it is advantageous to build large wind generators. However, it is hard to build a large vertical-axis generator that is both light enough to rotate in a light breeze and strong enough to stand up to strong winds. As a result, vertical-axis wind generators are generally not practical for generating enough electric power to make them economical to use.

Most research and testing today centers around horizontal-axis wind generators. Although these generators lose power when moving to point into the wind, they gain more than they lose because it is relatively easy to build large wind generators.

Usually, two or three blades are mounted on a rotating hub. A gearbox inside the hub transfers the rotational power to the generator. The blades look something like the blades of an airplane propeller but are long and slender. They can be tilted so that they can take the proper bite of the air no matter what the wind speed. Wind turbine blades 200 feet (about 60 m) and more in diameter are possible. A wind generator with a 200-foot diameter can generate sixteen times as much power as a wind generator that is 50 feet (about 15 m) in diameter.

To point horizontal-axis wind generators into the wind, a large fin sticks out from the back of the hub and works like a weather vane. A second way to point a wind generator is to design the blades so that they work downwind of the hub. The wind simply pushes the blades around until they move to the far side of the hub and start spinning.

Wind generators have three main drawbacks. First, they are expensive. Second, not all locations have consistent strong winds. In some places the wind rarely blows at all, making them bad sites for wind generators. Third, even in good locations, the wind will stop from time to time and sometimes it will blow so hard that the windmill blades will have to be adjusted so that they don't turn at all to prevent them from breaking. This means that wind generator users should have a backup system using some other kind of electric generation to provide electricity when the wind generator isn't working.

Though not practical in all locations, wind generators are a good idea in those areas where they can be used, because the wind is free. Wind generators do not pollute the air or produce radioactive wastes. The electricity they produce can be sent right into the electric power system to join electricity generated by other means. Some private wind generator owners, who use the wind and back it up with electricity from the power company, send their excess electricity on especially windy days into power company power lines. The private owner's electric meter reverses so that the monthly electric bill is reduced.

Wind generators produce only a tiny fraction of the electricity used in the United States every day.

HYDROELECTRIC POWER

The earth can be thought of as a giant heat engine. The sun heats the earth's surface, causing hot air to rise and cool air to move in to take its place. As we saw in the section on wind generators, this air movement can be put to use generating electricity. In addition to moving the air, the sun's heat also causes water to evaporate from the earth's surface. Water vapor eventually returns to the surface as rain. The rain collects in rivers that flow downward to the oceans. The energy in that flow can be used to generate electricity.

The energy of water running down steep river valleys can be captured by a special kind of waterwheel called a *turbine*. The turbine blades are enclosed so that most of the water that passes through their housing pushes the blades. A dam is erected across the valley to funnel the water through the turbine. It is called a *hydroelectric dam*. The energy caught by the turbine is then transferred by a rotating shaft to a magnetic electric generator to produce electricity.

In river valleys where the water is moving slowly, very large dams are erected. This produces a large and deep lake. Water behind the dam escapes through large pipes inside the dam walls themselves. Somewhere near the bottom, the pipes aim the fast-moving water at the turbines so that their energy is captured. The higher the dam, the greater the force of the water that pushes the turbine. More water pressure means that more electricity can be generated.

Hydroelectric dams can be desirable producers of electricity. They make no smoke or radioactivity. However, since a dam turns a river valley into a lake, it does significantly affect the environment. How much damage is done depends upon the particular site. The lake formed behind the dam can flood valuable farmland or destroy a beautiful wilderness area. Although hydroelectric lakes can be used for recreational boating, fishing, and swimming, they are often muddy because they trap sediment carried by the running water. Sometimes, recreational uses of the river after it passes through the dam are eliminated. A major potential problem is that hydroelectric dams can collapse and the rushing wall of water released can cause a great deal of destruction to the people and buildings located in the valley below.

Hydroelectric power accounts for about 12 to 14 percent of our electrical energy. Most usable big rivers already have dams on them. However, there are still sites on many small, fast-moving rivers that could be used to produce power.

EXPERIMENT:
BUILDING A WIND GENERATOR

MATERIALS

Small toy DC motor
Several feet of bell wire
Wood board, about 1 x 1 x 16 inches (2.5 x 2.5 x 41 cm)
Wood board, about 8 x 8 x 1 inches (20 x 20 x 2.5 cm)
Small pieces of lightweight wood or metal for making
    windmill blades
Volt-ohmmeter
Window fan

In this experiment you will have to make some construction decisions based on the materials you have at hand. Join the two boards together as shown in Fig. 10. Fasten the small motor at the top of the upright piece so that the motor shaft extends outward from the upright. You might want to use a metal strap or some strong tape to do this.

Make two blades out of a lightweight material. The blades should be about 12 inches (30 cm) in diameter when they are mounted to the motor. Mount the blades to the motor shaft. To do this, you might try drilling a hole in a small disk of wood just large enough for the hole to slip snugly over the motor shaft. Then attach the blades to the

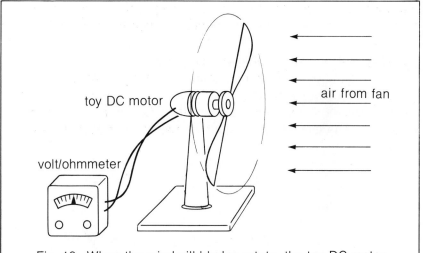

Fig. 10. When the windmill blades rotate, the toy DC motor becomes a generator and produces DC electricity, which is registered by the meter.

block. It is important that the blades be balanced so that they turn freely. It is also important that the blades be tilted like fan blades so that they will catch moving air and start moving themselves. Take a look at fan blades to see what is required.

Next, connect the wires from the motor to the meter. You will probably have to add bell wire here because motor lead wires are usually very short. Spin the blades gently with your fingers. If connected up properly, the needle in the meter will move, indicating electricity is being generated. If not, check your connections to the motor and meter to see if everything is properly set up. If working properly, direct the airflow from a window fan or take your windmill outside on a windy day.

This experiment gives you the opportunity to try different windmill blade designs. Do wide blades generate more electricity than narrow ones? Is two the best number for blades or is three or four better? How steeply should the blades be tilted to generate the most power?

Why is electricity being generated?

The blades of the windmill capture moving air and use it to turn the DC motor shaft. When you pass electricity through a DC motor, it turns. However, if you turn the shaft, the DC motor then becomes a generator. The electricity it produces makes the needle move.

CHEMICAL ELECTRICITY

Not all of the electricity we use comes from magnetic generators. When you start a car or turn on a flashlight, electricity is produced by chemicals. Chemicals also produce electricity for radios, wristwatches, and hearing aids and for pacemakers placed inside the human body for people who have heart problems.

WET CELLS AND DRY CELLS

The way electricity is extracted from chemicals is fairly easy to understand. First, a chemical cell is constructed. The cell is a container such as a glass that is filled with a solution of water and sulfuric acid. Inserted into the glass are two rods, one copper and the other zinc.

Immediately after inserting the rods, a chemical reaction begins. The copper reacts with the solution and begins to lose electrons so that it becomes positively charged. The zinc also begins to react and gains electrons so that it becomes negatively charged. The electrons lost from the copper actually travel through the solution to the zinc.

During the reaction, the copper develops such a strong positive charge that any electron (negative charge) released by it is immediately pulled back because of the attraction between positive and negative charges. The zinc develops such a strong negative charge that any new electrons are repelled by that charge. At this point, the chemical reactions stop. No electricity is being produced yet.

When a conducting wire is strung across the tops of the copper and zinc outside the cell itself, the reaction can begin again. The zinc has a new place for its electrons to go. The electrons travel through the wire to the copper. The copper loses its strong positive charge because of the new electrons and begins to react with the solution again as it did before. It will give up more electrons to the solution and these will travel to the zinc again. The electrons will go back out through the wire to the copper to begin the cycle all over. The electron flow is electricity that can be used to power a radio or a flashlight (Fig. 11).

The cell just described is called a *wet cell* because of the liquid acid and water solution inside. It has one big disadvantage. The solution can easily be spilled from it. The *dry cell*, though similar in nature, is much more convenient to use. This is the kind of cell used in flashlights and radios. Often, people mistakenly call dry cells "batteries." A *battery* is technically two or more cells working together. If your flashlight has two cells inside, you can call them a battery. Also, some cells come from the store already joined together. A 6-volt lantern battery actually has several small cells built inside, as does the 9-volt radio battery.

Dry cells are not really dry. They contain a moist, pasty acid solution. The container for the cell is made of the metal zinc. A rod of carbon is placed in the middle of the cell. As with wet cells, chemical reactions take place that release electrons from the carbon and give them to the zinc case. A wire connecting the zinc to the carbon outside the dry cell permits the electricity to flow.

The top of the dry cell is positive, and the bottom is negative. When two cells are added together to form the battery for a flashlight, the top of one cell touches the bottom of the other. Electricity passes from the bottom of the first cell into the top of the second. It continues through the second cell to its bottom and leaves to light the flashlight bulb. The electric current then enters the top of the cell

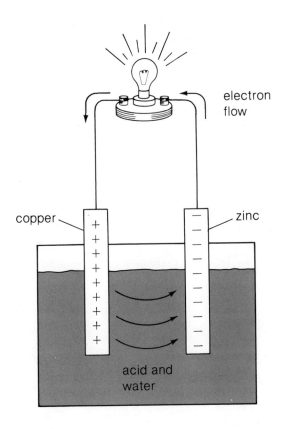

copper

electron
flow

zinc

acid and
water

Fig. 11. In this wet cell, electrons flow to the zinc electrode,
which becomes negative. The copper electrode then becomes
positive. Electrons begin a current, leaving the zinc electrode
through the wire and returning to the copper electrode.

to complete the circuit. The electricity produced by the second cell adds to that of the first so that the power is increased.

It would seem that chemical cells are the perfect electrical generators, but this is not entirely true. Eventually, the cells die because the chemicals are consumed. The zinc, in particular, is eaten away. In cheaper cells, this produces holes in the case allowing the gooey paste to leak out and moisture from the air to enter in. This expands the battery case and ruins the flashlight. Better flashlight cells have leakproof steel jackets that prevent this problem.

CAR BATTERIES

One other battery is worth describing here: the lead-acid automobile battery. This kind of battery has three or six wet cells made up of two kinds of lead and a sulfuric acid and water solution inside a plastic case. Each cell produces 2 volts of electricity, giving the battery either 6 or 12 volts. The case prevents the acid solution from spilling out.

This battery provides starting power for your car and for turning on the headlights and other electrical devices when the engine is not running. As with other batteries, some of the chemicals are consumed by producing electricity. However, while the car is running, a magnetic generator, powered by the engine, takes over producing the electricity needed for headlights and other electrical devices. It also sends electricity into the battery to recharge it by reversing the battery's chemical process. This prepares the battery for the next start.

Scientists in many locations are trying to develop new high-power, long-lasting batteries for all-electric cars. Electric cars are impractical right now because the batteries in use are heavy and require frequent charging.

FUEL CELLS

America's space program has led to the development of a special device to furnish electricity needed onboard manned spacecraft: the *fuel cell.* The fuel cell is a chemical battery that never wears out. Chemicals in dry and wet cells are eventually used up. The fuels for the fuel cell are hydrogen and oxygen gas that come from outside storage tanks. As long as hydrogen and oxygen are supplied, the fuel cell produces electricity.

During the hydrogen–oxygen reaction, water is formed as a by-product and has to be removed. NASA engineers, fighting weight and storage limitations aboard space capsules, use the waste water for drinking and washing water. This eliminated the need to carry large water tanks onboard for the astronauts. Fuel cells are still used in space today onboard the Space Shuttle. Waste water from fuel cells is used for cooling purposes.

NASA has sought to use its fuel cell technology on earth as well. Mobile-home–size fuel cells have been airlifted to disaster sites to provide emergency electric power.

A new generation of fuel cells is on the horizon that are being designed to run on oil or a modified coal. Such a system offers the possibility of cleanly converting oil or coal to useful electricity.

EXPERIMENT:
MAKING A
LEMON WET CELL

Wet cells can be made out of many materials. A very simple wet cell that actually works is made out of two wires and a lemon.

MATERIALS

Lemon or other citrus fruit
Volt-ohmmeter
Stiff copper wire
Large paper clip

Connect two pieces of copper wire to the terminals of the meter. If there is paint or insulation on the other ends of the wire, remove it.

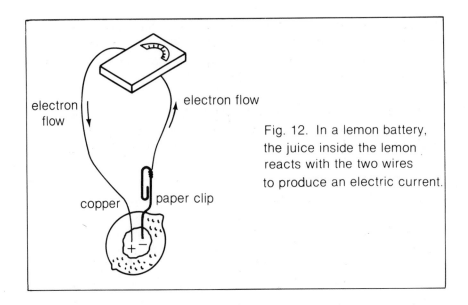

electron flow

electron flow

copper

paper clip

Fig. 12. In a lemon battery, the juice inside the lemon reacts with the two wires to produce an electric current.

Open up the paper clip and splice it to one of the wires (Fig. 12). Roll the lemon on a hard surface, pressing on it to break up some of the pulp and release the juice inside.

Insert the copper wire and the paper clip through the skin of the lemon and into the juice. Make sure the two wires are close to each other but not touching. Observe the meter.

How is the current produced?

The lemon acts as a wet cell. The juice inside the lemon is a mild acid. Chemical reactions with the two different metals and the lemon juice take electrons away from one wire and give them to the other. The electrons flow out of the lemon through the wire and through the meter and back inside the lemon by the other wire. This is the principle behind the way flashlight cells operate.

Try other citrus fruits and see how much electricity is produced. Will apples work? Try jelly, soda pop, and coffee or tea to see if they will work also. Will two lemons produce more electricity than one? Try rigging up two lemons.

UNUSUAL
GENERATORS

SOLAR CELLS

In most types of electrical generation, the action of chemicals or the motion of magnetic generators is used to produce electricity. Solar or photovoltaic cells take sunlight and convert it directly into electricity without chemical reactions or spinning magnetic generators.

Solar cells were invented at the Bell Telephone Laboratories in 1954. Their first important use was for making the electricity needed by satellites. Early satellites were powered by batteries. Unfortunately, batteries have a short life-span, which limited the life of the satellite. Solar cells were a great advancement in satellite technology because they produced electricity whenever a satellite was in the sunlight and they worked for years.

The solar cells used in the first satellites were expensive and inefficient. They cost in the neighborhood of $300 for each watt of power produced. (A *watt* is an electrical unit for power.) To put this in perspective, buying enough solar cells to generate electricity to light just one 100-watt light bulb cost $30,000! However, except for batteries, solar cells were the only devices available to power satellites. Therefore, solar cells were and continue to be used for many satellites. The only drawback for their use on satellites is that satellites pass within the earth's shadow for a part of each orbit, and the electricity generation stops. This problem is solved simply by including batteries on satellites. Excess electricity produced by the solar cells

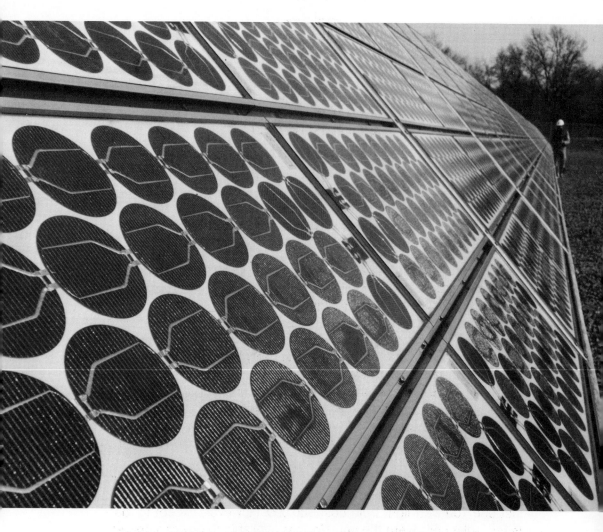

An array of solar cells in the Beverly High School Photovoltaic System in Beverly, Massachusetts. The 100,000-watt system uses over 3,200 modules, each containing 36 solar cells. The system will provide about 10 percent of the electricity needed by the school.

is sent to the batteries to recharge them for times when the solar cells are in the earth's shadow.

Solar cells work because there is energy in light. Under the right conditions, light falling on the surface of a particular material will dislodge electrons from the atoms that make up that material. If the electrons are collected by wires and made to run in a current, electricity is produced.

Solar cells come in many shapes and sizes. They can be round, rectangular, square, or pie-shaped. Each cell, however, is very flat and thin.

Solar cells are usually made up of crystals of the element silicon. Silicon is grown as a crystal from a molten solution. A small amount of boron is added to the solution.

When the crystal is cool, it is sliced to form thin wafers of silicon that look like thin cookies. Then, phosphorus is added to one side of each wafer. The phosphorus penetrates slightly into the surface, making each surface of the wafer different. One side has boron and the other phosphorus.

Because of the way silicon and boron combine, that side of the wafer has a shortage of electrons. The shortage is usually referred to as "holes," or places where electrons could go. Therefore, this side of the cell is considered electrically positive. The combination of phosphorus and silicon on the other side of the wafer provides extra electrons, making that side negative (Fig. 13).

With one side of the wafer positive and the other side negative, electrons begin to move to fill in the holes. However, the moment the nearest holes are filled, the movement stops because the filled holes prevent any more electrons from passing them by to the holes beyond. It's as though a fence has been set up. The result is that many holes beyond the "fence" are left unfilled.

To turn a silicon wafer into a solar cell, a fine grid of wires is placed on the top of the phosphorus side of the cell and a piece of metal is placed over the boron side of the cell. A wire is attached to the metal piece and a second wire to the wire grid. This completes the solar cell.

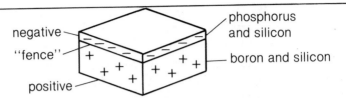

negative — "fence" — positive

phosphorus and silicon — boron and silicon

Fig. 13. When phosphorus is added to the top of a silicon wafer, extra electrons move toward the boron side. As soon as some "holes" in the boron side are filled, the electron flow stops. The filled holes act like a fence to keep other electrons out. The thickness of the wafer is greatly exaggerated. Solar cell wafers are usually only about as thick as several sheets of paper.

To make the solar cell work, the two wires are connected to an electrical device such as a motor. The wire grid side is placed in the sunlight and electricity begins traveling through the top wire to the motor, making it run, and back to the cell through the bottom wire. This happens because sunlight penetrates into the cell to where the "fence" is.

The energy in that light "kicks" the electrons from their holes and causes them to move to the top of the cell. The wire grid at the top collects the electrons, and they flow away to the motor and back to the bottom of the cell. Back inside the cell, the electrons are attracted back to the fence and are again kicked out the top. The electrons continue to circulate as long as the sunlight or other light continues to fall on the cell (Fig. 14). To increase the electricity output of solar cells, two or more cells are wired together in a manner similar to joining chemical dry cells.

Over the years, scientific research has improved the efficiency of solar cells and greatly reduced their cost by developing better manufacturing techniques. Solar cells are useful for electric power generation in remote parts of the world, where standard electric generation is very hard and expensive to come by. Solar cells are also

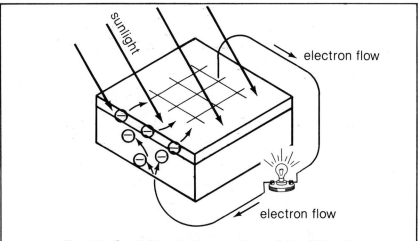

Fig. 14. Sunlight entering a solar cell top "kicks" electrons out of the "fence" and sends them through the wire grip to the bulb and back into the cell bottom.

used for quite a number of interesting applications, such as powering pocket calculators and watches. Large-scale solar cell generation of electricity is still a long way from becoming practical because the electricity from them still costs more than electricity from standard generators.

ANIMAL ELECTRICITY

When, in the nineteenth century, Luigi Galvani first observed the twitching of frog legs when they contacted two different metals, he wrongly concluded that the twitching was caused by "animal electricity." He was really observing the chemical battery effect. But he wasn't totally mistaken in believing in animal electricity because it does exist. The sensations of sight, touch, taste, smell, and hearing work because of electricity. Very weak electric currents carry messages along the nerves in your body. These signals are interpreted by your brain, and your brain sends other currents that tell your muscles when to do their jobs. However, another form of animal electricity also exists. It was known in ancient times.

Ancient Roman doctors were familiar with a sea ray fish that produced electric shocks when touched. Although the doctors did not understand what the shock was, they tried to put it to practical use by touching the ray to their patients. It is hard to say what the patients thought of the treatment, but the doctors felt that the shocks were of some benefit for a variety of ailments. Egyptians also knew of an electric animal, a catfish with an Arabic name that translates into "father of thunder." In South America, the most powerful of all electric animals, the electric eel, was known before the arrival of European explorers. It lived in the rivers there, and when someone accidentally touched one, he felt a powerful shock that could stun or even kill him.

Today, ten families of fishes are known to produce electric shocks of different magnitudes. The electric rays, or torpedos, live along the bottom of shallow waters in the ocean. They are slow-moving and if you step on one, you can receive a shock of 220 volts. The electric catfish that live in murky waters in African rivers can grow to more than a yard (about 1 m) in length and deliver 350-volt shocks. The Amazon electric eel can be three times as long and can put out electric punches up to 650 volts, although 350 volts is more usual.

The different electric fish each have electric organs made up of special cells called *electrocytes*. The cells can be stacked one on top of another similar to voltaic cells. Electric eels have three such organs that contain several hundred thousand electrocytes that produce electricity. The currents flow in one direction along the organ and return through the surrounding water. If someone touches the organ, the current will go through him as well.

Electric fishes use their electricity for hunting. The shock stuns their prey. Shocks can also be used as a protection against intruders that come too close or that might want to eat them.

THERMOCOUPLES

With batteries and solar cells we have learned that some materials easily give up their electrons under the right conditions. If two wires made of different metals, such as copper and zinc, are brought together and heated, electricity is produced. The device is called a *thermocouple*.

Thermocouples produce electricity directly from heat without converting the heat into steam first. This happens because the copper wire gives up some of its electrons when it is heated and these electrons flow into the zinc wire. If an electric meter is connected to the other ends of the two wires, the electrons will flow through the meter, causing its needle to move, and back into the copper wire. The electric current produced by a thermocouple is weak but can be strengthened by adding more thermocouples together to form a *thermopile*.

Because thermocouples produce only weak currents, they are not being put to use in generating useful quantities of electricity, although further research into them does offer some potential for the future. Today, thermocouples are used as a part of high-temperature thermometers. The electrical output of a thermocouple changes with temperature, and a meter connected to a thermocouple will convert the current to a temperature reading.

ELECTRICITY FROM PRESSURE

A very simple form of electrical generation comes from pressure. Pushing or pounding on some crystals and certain ceramic materials causes electrons in their atoms to move. The electrons move from one side of the material to the other. When the pressure is let up, the electrons return. The electricity produced in this manner is called *piezoelectricity*. *Piezo* is a Greek word that means "to press."

Piezoelectricity is of limited use when compared with the other forms of electric generation. Still, it does have its use. Some phonograph arms convert to an electric current the pressures felt by the needle, mounted on a crystal, as it hits the tiny bumps in the record grooves. The current is then amplified into sound. Some microphones also use a crystal to convert the pressure of sound waves into an electric current. A pressure on a crystal in another device produces an electric spark that lights a gas charcoal grill or a gas clothes drier.

EXPERIMENT:
USING SOLAR CELLS

Solar cells are easy to experiment with because they come ready to use. It is merely a matter of connecting them to a motor or some other device.

MATERIALS

Several solar cells (The number of cells will depend upon the kind you use. They can be purchased from electronic supply stores, or perhaps your school will have some that you can borrow.)
Volt-ohmmeter
Bell wire
Tape

Connect two wires to each cell. Some cells do not come with wires attached so you will have to tape one wire to the metal bottom of each cell and one to the contact where all the thin wires of the top merge to a point. Attach the other ends of the wires to the meter, and measure the cell's output when the cell is exposed to strong light such as from the sun.

Try a second experiment by joining several cells together. Splice the wire from the bottom of one cell to the wire from the top of another. Follow this procedure until all cells are joined together, but leave the last two wires unconnected. Connect these wires to the meter. Now, expose the cells to strong light and measure the output of the cells.

Try a similar experiment but this time splice all the wires from the bottoms of the cells together in one group and all the wires from the tops in another. Again attach the meter and measure the output.

Try attaching the wires to a toy DC motor. If you have a toy car or other toy that is run by batteries, use the cells in place of the batteries.

Why is there a difference in the electricity produced when the cells are hooked up in different ways?

One solar cell will produce a certain voltage and current. Two cells will either double the voltage current or increase the amount of current that can be drawn. A series hookup (the first one you tried) increases the voltage produced while the current remains the same. The second hookup was a parallel circuit that keeps the voltage the same but increases the current produced.

EXPERIMENT:
MAKING A
THERMOCOUPLE

By twisting together two different wires, a thermocouple that will produce a small amount of electricity can quickly be made.

MATERIALS

Copper wire
Iron picture-hanger wire
Candle and matches
Volt-ohmmeter

Scrape off several inches of insulation or paint on the ends of the two wires. Twist the ends of the copper and iron wires together as shown in Fig. 15. Connect their other ends to the meter. Light the candle and hold the twisted wires in the flame. Watch the meter. Be careful, the wires will soon get hot and could burn your fingers!

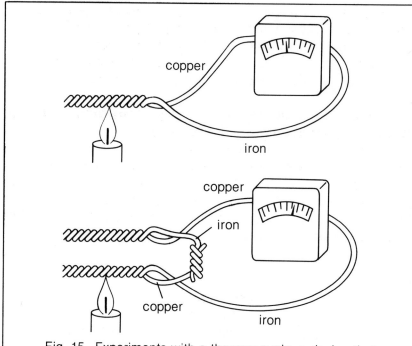

Fig. 15. Experiments with a thermocouple, a device that converts heat energy to electrical energy. In the first experiment (top), a simple thermocouple is made from wires made of copper and iron. In the second experiment (below), two thermocouples are connected together to increase the output of electricity.

Try a second experiment by twisting two sets of wires and holding both in the flame.

Why is electricity produced?

When two different metals are brought in contact and heated, electrons are released from one metal and given to the other. This starts a current that flows through the meter.

ON THE
HORIZON

As we have seen, electricity can be generated in many ways. New ways are being thought of all the time, and the old ways are continually being improved.

Magnetic generators, for instance, lose some of the power they produce because the wires that make up their coils turn some of the energy in the electricity passing through them to heat. Scientists have learned that some materials produce more heat from electricity than others. They also have learned that the amount of energy lost depends upon the temperature of the wires. Wires kept at a very low temperature produce little heat from electricity.

Knowing this, new generators are being developed to operate at supercold temperatures. Special metals are used for the wire coils and are bathed in liquid helium. Helium is a gas at normal temperatures but becomes a liquid when cooled to minus 425 degrees Fahrenheit (minus 218 degrees Celsius). The low operating temperature reduces energy loss in generators, boosting their overall efficiency to nearly 99 percent.

Another generating process, called *magnetohydrodynamics* (MHD), shows much promise for the future. Actually, MHD has been under research for at least four decades. The process uses coal for producing electricity. Coal is burned to heat air to an extremely high temperature of 4,000 to 5,000 degrees Fahrenheit (2,200 to 2,700 degrees Celsius). The hot air is seeded with the element potassium, and this makes the air electrically conductive. The air is then passed through a long tunnel called the MHD box. A powerful magnet surrounds this box. The conducting air expands as it races through the tunnel. In the process, a strong electric current is transferred from the air to conducting wires lining the tunnel.

MHD can be combined with a standard steam generating plant. The superhot air passing through the tunnel can be directed to a boiler, where the heat will produce steam. That steam drives turbines, which then turn magnetic generators. With MHD added to a steam plant, an additional 20 percent of the available energy from burning coal can be used.

Another method would use temperature differences in the oceans to produce electricity. In many parts of the ocean, the surface water is relatively warm and the deep water is relatively cold. The temperature differences could be taken advantage of by constructing a floating platform with a large tube extending down into the cold water. The heat in the surface water is used to boil special low-temperature liquids. The steam produced drives turbines and so on. Cool water, brought up from the depths, condenses the steam and starts the process all over again.

An even more exciting proposal for generating electricity takes us out into space. The sun releases huge amounts of energy into space. At 93 million miles (about 150 million km) away, the earth receives only one two-billionth of that energy, but not all that energy actually reaches the earth's surface. Some of it is reflected back into space by clouds. What does get through makes life possible on earth. Using solar energy on earth is a great idea, but, you will remember, this energy form is hampered by a couple of problems. Clouds reduce the amount of sunlight that reaches the earth's surface, and on very cloudy days, solar generating equipment is of little use. Furthermore, nightfall stops all electricity production. However, if a solar electricity plant were orbiting in space, these problems would disappear.

Scientists have proposed constructing large platforms in space. Parts for these platforms would be carried to orbit by the Space Shuttle. There, space hard-hat workers would assemble the parts into a large, flat surface possibly 25 square miles (68 sq km) in area.

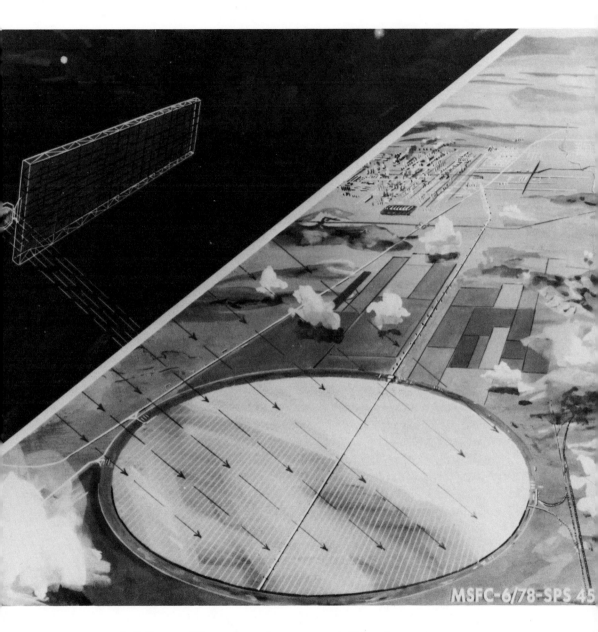

Artist's rendition of a solar power platform in space.

The surface of the platform would be aimed at the sun and would be covered with solar cells. Electricity produced by the cells would be converted into laser beams or microwaves and transmitted to earth, where receivers would convert the energy back into electricity.

One other electricity producer for the future should be mentioned, *fusion.* Earlier, nuclear fission was described. With fission, atoms are split and the heat released can be converted into electricity through a steam generator. Fusion is also an atomic process, but unlike fission, atoms undergoing fusion are fused or joined together. During the fusion process tremendous amounts of heat are released. This heat can be used to generate electricity.

Fusion is the same process the sun uses to make its energy. Deuterium and tritium, two varieties of the element hydrogen, are suitable as fusion fuel. When they are fused, the element helium is produced, as well as heat energy. To achieve fusion, tritium and deuterium have to be compressed and heated to temperatures three times hotter than the interior of the sun. At this temperature, the atoms try to move away from one another, stopping the reaction. One scheme to keep them together is to hold them with a powerful magnetic field. Still another method is bombarding tritium and deuterium pellets with lasers, which heat the pellets.

To make fusion worthwhile, more heat has to be released than was used to start the fusion process. The extra heat produced will be used to produce steam for magnetic generators. In some experiments, lasting for only a fraction of a second, break-even has been achieved, but we are still a long way from producing large amounts of heat on a continual basis. Fusion will most likely be a process for producing electricity in the twenty-first century. One of the great promises fusion holds is that the fuel to feed the process is plentiful on earth in the oceans.

PAST, PRESENT, AND FUTURE

The world of today is very different from the world of a hundred years ago. Back then, people didn't use electricity often. To do any job required human or animal muscle power, steam engines, or water power. Factory workers were limited in what they could produce in a day. Travel took days instead of hours or minutes. Communication between great distances was a slow process. Homes were lit by gas lamps.

Today, we take much for granted. But if it weren't for electricity, life would be very different. There would be no electric motors, telephones, and television. Automobiles and factories would run on steam power. Life today would not be significantly different from that in the 1880s.

Life has changed so dramatically in the last hundred years because of the availability of electricity. We have so many ways of generating electricity and transporting it to where it is needed that its use has become as commonplace as eating and sleeping. With new technologies for generating electricity and for improving the ways of generating we have now, we may reach a time when we will have all the electricity we will ever need. Assuming this happens, try to imagine what our world will be like a hundred years from now.

GLOSSARY

Alternating Current—Electricity that reverses direction periodically.

Battery—Two or more wet or dry cells connected together.

Brushes—Small pieces of metal that brush against the rotating wire coil of a magnetic generator to draw off a current.

Coal Gasification—A process in which coal is turned into a gas for use in gas furnaces.

Direct Current—Electricity that travels in one direction only.

Dry Cell—A chemical cell for producing electricity in which the moist, pasty chemicals inside are sealed within a case to prevent leakage or spilling.

Electric Current—Electricity transferred from one place to another by a flow of electrons.

Electrocytes—In certain animals, an organ composed of special cells that produce a strong current of electricity for use in hunting and defense.

Fission—An atomic reaction in which large atoms are split to produce smaller atoms and release heat that can be used for generating electricity.

Fuel Cell—An electricity-producing device that combines oxygen and hydrogen from outside supply tanks to make electricity.

Fusion—An atomic reaction in which small atoms are fused to produce larger atoms and in doing so release heat that may someday be used to generate electricity.

Geothermal Heat—Heat produced in the interior of the earth from the pressure of rock lying on top of rock and from radioactive decay of some elements.

Heliostat—A movable mirror used to concentrate sunlight in a solar furnace.

Hydroelectric Dam—A river dam that directs water through turbines connected to electric generators so that the energy in the moving water can produce electricity.

Liquefaction—A process that turns coal into oil for burning in oil furnaces.

Magnetic Generator—An electric generator in which a coil of wire moves within a strong magnetic field and produces electricity.

Magnetohydrodynamics—A process for producing electricity in which air is heated to a very high temperature and passed through a magnetic field.

Piezoelectricity—Electricity produced by pressure on certain crystals.

Reactor—The apparatus in which fission takes place.

Static Electricity—A form of electricity in which a charge comes to rest on the surface of some object.

Thermocouple—A device consisting of two different metals that produce electricity directly from heat.

Thermopile—Two or more thermocouples connected together.

Turbine—Waterwheel-like devices that capture the energy of steam or running water and convert it to rotary motion.

Watt—The electrical unit for power—how much work is done each second.

Wet Cell—A cell that produces electricity from wet chemicals.

BIBLIOGRAPHY

Ardley, Neil. *Discovering Electricity.* New York: Watts, 1984.

Asimov, Isaac. *How Did We Find Out About Solar Power.* New York: Walker, 1981.

Branley, Franklin M. *Energy for the Twenty-First Century.* New York: Harper & Row, 1975.

Carey, Helen H. *Producing Energy.* New York: Watts, 1984.

Goldin, Augusta. *Geothermal Energy: A Hot Prospect.* San Diego, Calif.: Harcourt Brace, 1981.

Lampton, Christopher. *Fusion: The Eternal Flame.* New York: Watts, 1982.

Leon, George deLucenay. *Energy Forever: Power for Today and Tomorrow.* New York: Arco, 1981.

Math, Irwin. *Understanding and Using Electricity.* New York: Scribner, 1981.

Payne, Sherry. *Wind and Water Energy.* Milwaukee, Wisc.: Raintree, 1983.

Spooner, Maggie. *Sunpower Experiments.* New York: Sterling, 1979.

Watson, Jane W. *Alternate Energy Sources.* New York: Watts, 1979.

INDEX